SPOTLIGHT ON EXPLORERS AND COLONIZATION™

JUAN PONCE DE LEÓN

First Explorer of Florida and First Governor of Puerto Rico

HEATHER MOORE NIVER

New York

Published in 2017 by The Rosen Publishing Group, Inc.
29 East 21st Street, New York, NY 10010

First Edition

Library of Congress Cataloging-in-Publication Data

Names: Niver, Heather Moore, author.
Title: Juan Ponce de León : first explorer of Florida and first governor of Puerto Rico / Heather Moore Niver.
Description: First edition. | New York : Rosen Publishing, 2017. | Series: Spotlight on explorers and colonization | Includes bibliographical references and index. | Audience: Grade 7 to 12.
Identifiers: LCCN 2016000106| ISBN 9781477788202 (library bound) | ISBN 9781477788189 (pbk.) | ISBN 9781477788196 (6-pack)
Subjects: LCSH: Ponce de León, Juan, 1460?–1521. |
Explorers—America—Biography. | Explorers—Spain—Biography. |
Florida—Discovery and exploration—Spanish. | America—Discovery and exploration—Spanish.
Classification: LCC E125.P7 N58 2016 | DDC 910.92—dc23
LC record available at http://lccn.loc.gov/2016000106

Manufactured in the United States of America

CONTENTS

THE LONG LIFE OF A TALL TALE

It's a hopeful story: the discovery of a fountain that, with one dip into its waters, turns the old and ailing back into young, energetic people. It's such a terrific tale that it has lasted from ancient times and transformed from myth into an indelible part of history. Juan Ponce de León is the Spanish explorer who is credited with seeking this fictitious fountain. But the truth is that the multiple voyages he made throughout his life had nothing to do with a fountain at all. But because no one can resist a story of hope and rejuvenation, the

explorer's association with the Fountain of Youth remains to this day.

In reality, Ponce de León was one of Spain's first explorers of the New World. He was the first to officially discover the state of Florida. He was a skilled explorer and businessman, but, like many during his time, his expeditions were often focused on finding gold and taking slaves.

EARLY MYSTERIES

Juan Ponce de León was born in the village of San Tervás de Campos, Spain. It is in an area that is now known as Valladolid. There has been some question about which year he came into the world. For years, sources insisted that he was born in 1460, but 1474 is now accepted. Researchers eventually found a court document in which Juan Ponce de León stated that he was forty years old in 1514. Yet another researcher argues a third birth year of 1469, citing another court document. However, no one else has been able to access the record.

Ponce de León's immediate family is a bit of a mystery, too, because of extremely limited documentation. Historians aren't sure

who his parents were, but they appear to have been members of the nobility. Other sources claim he came from a poor family, citing this as a reason some of his expeditions were focused on gaining gold. Still others state that his family was a part of the nobility but were still poor.

This portrait of Ferdinand II of Aragon, also known as Ferdinand the Catholic, was painted by the Dutch painter Michiel Sittow.

Juan Ponce de León may have been related to Rodrigo Ponce de León, who was the Duke of Cádiz. Rodrigo Ponce de León was renowned for his acts in the Reconquista. The Reconquista was the series of battles between Christian and Muslim kingdoms for control of the Iberian Peninsula. It lasted hundreds of years and ended when the Moors, as the Muslim rulers of Spain were called, were forced out of Granada in 1492.

Early on, before his days as an explorer, Ponce de Léon had a few different jobs. Some of these gave him experiences he was able to use when he was sailing the seas. At age eight or ten, Ponce de Léon became a page at the court of Aragon, for a Spanish knight known as Pedro Núñez de Guzmán. He worked for a prince as well, who would become Ferdinand II of Aragon. His work taught him important social skills, religious customs, and military strategies. At eighteen, he fought in several wars for Spain, which may have given him excellent experience as a soldier.

SAILING WITH COLUMBUS

Many explorers were poor and set off in search of riches. But Ponce de León may have joined the ranks of explorers simply because he was curious and adventurous. In 1493, he was a part of Christopher Columbus's second voyage to the New World. Columbus's initial voyage was rumored to have been very fruitful, with talk of gold, valuable stones, and spices, all easily obtained. With a record like that, he had many eager volunteers on his second voyage. Ponce de León was listed as one of two hundred "gentlemen volunteers"— mostly Spanish sailors, soldiers, and settlers who took part. The seventeen ships making

CHRISTOPHER COLUMBUS.

up the expedition set sail on September 25.

The ships arrived in the Caribbean in November. After stopping at several islands, they finally arrived on an island Columbus called Isle of Spain, or Hispaniola. (Today the island is divided into two nations: Haiti and the Dominican Republic.) During this voyage, members of the expeditions also founded a settlement called La Isabela on the island.

Columbus's main goal for his second trip across the Atlantic was not exploration, as it had been during his 1492 voyage, but colonization. The

Taíno natives were friendly and generous, even showing their new visitors where to find gold in the river and offering them as much as they liked. Before long, however, the Spaniards forced native Indians into slavery.

The voyage was not easy for the crew. Ponce de León and the others suffered from diseases, dreadful weather, and too little food and drink. Records also suggest that this voyage was not as well prepared for as Columbus's famous 1492 trip. In fact, it appears to have been such a mess that many of the volunteers, who were previously enthusiastic, headed back home to Spain as soon as they could. Ponce de León seems to have been among them. Evidently, Columbus was a terrific explorer but not such a fabulous administrator for this voyage.

O, CAPTAIN! O, GOVERNOR!

After this voyage, Ponce de León likely returned to Spain and started making plans to set sail again. On February 13, 1502, he sailed with Nicolás de Ovando, who had been selected as governor of an area of several islands referred to as "the Indies." Ovando had been given an order from the king of Spain to conquer the native Taínos.

When the crew reached the Canary Islands, they decided to split up. One group sailed on and landed at the settlement of Santo Domingo, on Hispaniola, on April 15, 1502. Ponce de León lived on the island for the next two years. He spent several years conquering the people who lived here. When they (understandably) put up a fight against

the Spanish, Ponce de León and his crew slaughtered many of them. The acts were so violent that some consider them a massacre. Ponce de León's actions impressed Ovando, however, who named him provisionary governor of what is now the Dominican Republic.

RICH PORT

In 1505, Ponce de León established a new town called Salvaleón, where he would live for the next three years. He married a woman named Leónora. They would have three daughters—named Juana, Isabel, and María—and one son—named Luis.

In 1508, Ponce de León requested permission from Spain to sail to and take over a nearby island. The Spanish called the island San Juan Bautista (which is Spanish for "Saint John the Baptist), while the native people called it Borikén (which is Taíno for "Land of the Valiant Lord"). Today we know it as Puerto Rico. Some sources suggest that Ponce de León, who was an enthusiastic explorer, had already investigated the island on his own.

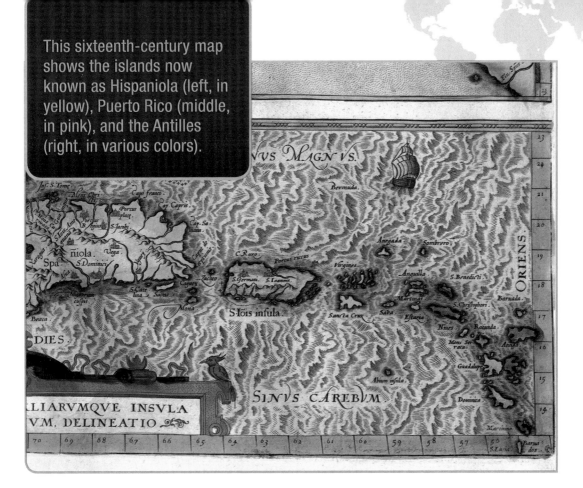

This sixteenth-century map shows the islands now known as Hispaniola (left, in yellow), Puerto Rico (middle, in pink), and the Antilles (right, in various colors).

After Ovando granted his request, Ponce de León arrived on the island with fifty soldiers and many settlers. They named the good harbor they discovered Puerto Rico (Spanish for "rich or fine port"). Ponce de León established a settlement there, which he named Caparra. Caparra was not an ideal site. Ponce de León was eventually forced to move the settlement to a barrier island near the coast. The modern-day city of San Juan is near this site.

This nineteenth-century illlustration is of Christopher Columbus's oldest son, Diego. The family's last name is Colón in Spanish and Colombo in its original Italian form.

At first, the native Taínos and their leader, the cacique (or chief) Agüeybaná, warmly greeted the Spaniards and welcomed them to the island. But before long, Ponce de León and the other settlers began suppressing the natives. It took less than a year for them to conquer the island and to subjugate most of the population. As a reward for this victory, Ovando named Ponce de León the captain-general and governor of the island.

Ponce de León's treatment of the natives has long been a topic of debate. Some say he was uncommonly kind to them and did not use violence. Others say he was very cruel, which resulted in his being removed from his position. It's possible that Ponce de León and his people killed so many of the Taínos that their actions there could be considered genocide against the natives. In fact, this may have been the reason that Diego Columbus, the oldest son of Christopher Columbus, replaced Ponce de León as governor in 1511.

FINDING FLORIDA

As soon as he was relieved of his position as governor, Ponce de León made plans to explore the nearby islands of Bimini, which are north of Cuba. The Spanish king, Ferdinand II, granted him the rights to and lifetime governorship of any islands he discovered. Ponce de León would still have to pay for the expedition himself, though.

Ponce de León set off from Puerto Rico with three ships on March 3, 1513. After sailing through some bad weather, they landed on April 2. We are not positive exactly where they landed, but it may have been slightly north of what we now know as Saint Augustine, Florida. Because he found

These bright blooms in a Florida park are an example of the many flowering plants that earned Florida the name Tierra La Florida, or "land of flowers."

the land on Easter Sunday (which is known as *Pascua Florida* in Spanish) and because he was impressed by its marvelous flowers, Ponce de León named it Tierra La Florida (which means "land of flowers"). So many Europeans had already landed here that the natives greeted them in Spanish! Ponce de León did not know that he was on the mainland of North America. He thought that he had landed on yet another island.

It wasn't until after his death that Ponce de León became entangled in rumors that he was searching for the fabled Fountain of Youth, as illustrated here.

JUAN PONCE DE LEON,
SEARCHING FOR THE FOUNTAIN OF YOUTH.

Was Ponce de León really looking for a fountain of youth? Some speculate that Ponce de León's goal on this trip was to find a rumored fountain that would grant the drinker a lifetime of youth. Records show that this probably wasn't his aim. His contracts for the expedition did not mention any such thing. In fact, his name wasn't even connected to it until after his death.

The earliest reference to Juan Ponce de León's association with the fabled fountain probably comes from 1575, when the Spaniard Hernando de Escalante Fontaneda wrote a memoir about the seventeen years he spent as a captive of the Calusa people of Florida. When Fontaneda was only thirteen years old, he was shipwrecked on Florida and held captive. In his memoir, he discusses how the Calusa talked about a magical river that turned old men into young men after a short dip in its waters. However, Fontaneda reported that, "to my great displeasure, I was never able to verify the fountain's existence."

RUMORS AND MORE

Gonzalo Fernández de Oviedo y Valdés also linked Juan Ponce de León with the legendary fountain of youth. This Spanish historian wrote about the explorers who made discoveries in the New World in his multivolume history, *General and Natural History of the Indies*. Although he penned glowing words about Columbus and Hernando Cortés, Oviedo thought other explorers, Ponce de León included, were greedy, vile, and foolish.

Oviedo thought that Ponce de León's only goal in exploration was to enhance his own ego, no matter how foolish the mission. He used the Fountain of Youth as his prime example of how gullible the explorer was,

Coronica delas Indias.

¶ La hystoria general de las Indias agora nueuamente im pressa corregida y emendada.

1547

stating that Indians in the Caribbean convinced the unwitting Ponce de León that the fountain was real. Oviedo claimed that Ponce de León led his expedition on a wild goose chase throughout the island for six months.

The Fountain of Youth Archaeological Park in St. Augustine, Florida, features a spring that is advertised as the Fountain of Youth.

The Spaniard Antonio de Herrera y Tordesillas offered an even more detailed version of the story in 1601. His work

may have been based on original accounts of the expedition that have been lost, but he was also a well-known plagiarist. Plagiarism was common at the time, and he may have "borrowed" heavily from Oviedo's and Fontaneda's versions of the story.

Another argument against Ponce de León having made such a search is that he wasn't an old man when he landed in Florida. However, the writer Washington Irving portrayed Ponce de León as an old man in a story he wrote nearly three hundred years later. Irving solidified the imagery of this story in the 1880s by erecting the lavish Ponce de Léon Hotel in Saint Augustine. (The Spanish, on the other hand, apparently never named anything after Ponce de León.)

In the 1920s, a man named Walter Fraser bought some land in St. Augustine's swampland. He found an old desecrated graveyard there and turned it into a Fountain of Youth attraction for tourists and kids.

NOT A NEW DISCOVERY

Although Ponce de León was the first to officially discover Florida, he was not the first person there. When Ponce de León arrived in Florida, it was already inhabited and had been for some time. Native Americans probably lived there as early as twelve thousand years ago.

By the first decade of the sixteenth century, points of land that likely represent Florida were appearing on maps from Europe. Before Ponce de León, navigators from Portugal or English sailors had probably found Florida first. Some historians argue that the explorer John Cabot, together with his teenaged son Sebastian, traveled down the state's east coast to Cape Florida in 1497.

Spanish expeditions in search of slaves had already been to the Bahamas, and it is likely they landed in Florida as well. It's possible that the less-than-welcome greeting that Ponce de León and his crew experienced was a result of the prior visits from slave traders.

Many Native Americans, such as the Timucua people shown in this engraving by Theodor be Bry, lived in Florida in the sixteenth century.

CURRENTS, MARTYRS, AND TORTOISES

After making landfall in Florida, the Ponce de León crew sailed down the coast. They passed one area that Ponce de León named Cabo de Corrientes (or "Cape of Currents"), which people think might have been Cape Canaveral. They continued south to discover the Bahama Channel. This turned out to be an important discovery because it revealed a new way to travel from Spain to the West Indies. He also sailed through the islands now known as the Florida Keys, which he named the Martyrs. He continued up along Florida's west coast before turning around near Pensacola Bay.

Sailing back south, the ships came to a group of islands. Ponce de León and his party needed to restock their food supply, so they stopped on one of the islands to hunt for sea turtles and seals. He named the island *Tortugas* (which means "tortoises") after all those turtles. Today the group of islands is known as the Dry Tortugas. The "dry" comes from the complete lack of fresh water on the island.

PUERTO RICO IN CHAOS

Ponce de León and his crew returned to Puerto Rico on September 21, 1513. Some reports say that he found the island in chaos and his house burned. His family had barely escaped! While they were gone, the formerly friendly Taínos had revolted.

At first the Taínos didn't think they could overtake the Spaniards, believing them to be immortal. The Taínos were forced to work as slaves in mines and fields. Taíno women were kidnapped. The Europeans took over the Taínos' land and brought with them new, terrible diseases that killed many natives. When a Taíno managed to drown a Spaniard, the natives realized the Spaniards were mortal. They fought back with

The gun that the Spanish soldier in this picture is holding is called an arquebus. The Spanish had more powerful weapons than the Taínos did.

whatever they had: wooden weapons, axes, and arrows.

Although they put up a good fight, the Spanish had superior weapons. Many Taínos escaped to nearby Caribbean islands called the Lesser Antilles. They joined South American tribes who had previously been their enemies in order to fight against the Europeans in Puerto Rico for the next twenty-five years.

BACK TO SPAIN

By 1514, Ponce de León was back in Spain reporting on his expedition. After describing his successes on Puerto Rico, he received many honors from King Ferdinand. He was knighted and granted his very own coat of arms—a shield representing Ponce de León and his family. He was also given a special title: Adelantado Don Juan Ponce de León. This meant he was the governor of the Islands of Bimini and Florida.

Ferdinand was so impressed with Ponce de León that he gave him a patent, or official permission, to sail back to Florida, on September 27, 1514. Once there, he was to explore the land and colonize it with Europeans. Permission for this trip may have been in part thanks to Ponce de León's

634. Ponce de León

635. Ponce de León

Among many honors he received from King Ferdinand, Ponce de León was granted a coat of arms, which was a shield design that represented his family name.

friendship with the influential Pedro Núñez de Guzmán. He was also ordered to subdue the natives there. Juan Ponce de León and his crew sailed the seas and headed back to Puerto Rico.

THE FATAL SHOT

Ponce de León seems to have spent some time in Puerto Rico before officially heading to Florida again. His ships finally set sail for Florida in 1521. After a rough, stormy trip, Ponce de León finally made his second landfall in Florida later that year. He arrived with two ships, two hundred people, fifty horses, and other domestic animals and tools for farming. They were ready to put down roots for a settlement. He may have brought priests with him, too, possibly with the idea of converting the natives. Records for this trip are limited, but some historians speculate that the expedition was not particularly well organized.

Crew and animals made landfall on Florida's west coast near Sanibel Island. They were busy building new homes to live in when natives attacked them. During this skirmish Ponce de León was injured in the thigh by an arrow, which may have been poisoned.

This eighteenth-century engraving depicts Ponce de León battling with the natives of Florida. His attempt to settle there in 1521 was met with attacks from the native people.

Ponce de León's tomb is in the Cathedral of San Juan Bautista, in San Juan, Puerto Rico. His remains were moved there in the early twentieth century.

This battle was the first of a three-hundred-year-long war against the natives on the North American continent; a war that amounted to ethnic cleansing of the native peoples. More

Europeans died in the pursuit of conquering Florida than in all the fights with natives in the west.

It wasn't long before the settlement was abandoned and the crew headed out. They appear to have gone to Havana, Cuba, where Ponce de León spent his last days. His wound should not have been life threatening, but unfortunately the Spanish at that time were unaware of the dangers of sepsis. Ponce de León drew his last breath in Cuba, dying from an infection in his wound and the resultant fever. He was probably only about forty-seven years old. His grave is in San Juan with the inscription, "Here rest the bones of a valiant LION, mightier in deeds than in name." *León* means "lion" in Spanish.

FACT AND FICTION

Despite recent attempts to sort out truth from fiction, the fiction seems to outweigh the facts. In 2013, Florida celebrated the five hundredth anniversary of Ponce de León's landing. As you can imagine, the Fountain of Youth story was a big part of that celebration. An enormous statue memorializing Juan Ponce de León looms in Florida's Melborne Beach, and the postal service issued a set of four stamps called "La Florida." Although his actual discoveries in and around the state are important, some critics worry that the rumors-turned-history based around the Fountain of Youth may overshadow the true events.

Although recent research shows that Ponce de León was not looking for the Fountain of Youth, his name may forever be associated with this fascinating fable.

The voyages of Juan Ponce de León helped expand the European understanding of the New World. He was responsible for the first European settlement on Puerto Rico. His discovery of the Bahama Channel changed travel for the Europeans. But unfortunately his name will forever be associated with the foolish search for a fictitious fountain of youth.

GLOSSARY

administrator A person whose job is to manage or run something.

barrier island A long, thin island that sits close to a mainland, protecting it from destruction and storms.

coat of arms A shield design representing a person, family, or country.

colonization The taking control and settling of a new place with people from another area.

genocide The methodical killing of a specific group of people.

gullible Made to believe something without difficulty.

inscription Words written permanently or carved into a gravestone or book.

knighted Officially made someone a knight.

nobility A group of people who are a part of the noble class, often with honorary titles.

page A young man in training to become a knight.

patent The official government permission that prevents others from doing or making something.

plagiarist A person who passed off the work or ideas of someone else as their own.

provisionary Temporary, for the current time.

rejuvenation To cause a person or thing to seem or feel younger or more energetic.

sepsis An infection of a wound from harmful bacteria.

speculate To think or guess about something.

subdue To force people or a country under control.

subjugate To bring someone or something under control or command, often by force.

The Explorers Club
46 East 70th Street
New York, NY 10021
(212) 628-8383
Website: https://explorers.org
Founded in in 1904, this organization seeks to uphold
    scientific exploration of all mediums by endorsing
    study and instruction in physical, natural, and
    biological sciences.

The Gilder Lehrman Institute of American History
49 West 45th Street, 6th floor
New York, NY 10036
(646) 366-9666
Website: https://www.gilderlehrman.org
The Gilder Lehrman Institute of American History is
    a nonprofit organization dedicated to improving
    history education through programs for teachers
    and students.

The Mariners' Museum
100 Museum Drive
Newport News, VA 23606
(757) 596-2222
Website: http://www.marinersmuseum.org
The Mariners' Museum uses art and relics to teach
    people about the importance of the sea in the
    advancement of humankind. It celebrates "the
    maritime world—past, present and future."

Royal Order of Ponce de León Conquistadors
PO Box 510664
Punta Gorda, FL 33951
Website: http://conquistadors-florida.com
The Royal Order of Ponce de León seeks to maintain
    the Spanish legacy of Charlotte County and Florida
    by celebrating Ponce de León's discovery and
    naming of Florida. It hopes to stimulate cultural
    and historical origins within the population.

Websites

Because of the changing nature of Internet links,
Rosen Publishing has developed an online list of
websites related to the subject of this book. This site
is updated regularly. Please use this link to access
the list:

http://www.rosenlinks.com/SEC/leon

Anderson, Marilyn. *Biographies of the New World*. New York, NY: Britannica Educational Publishing, 2013.

Eagen, Rachel. *Ponce De León: Exploring Florida and Puerto Rico.* Paradise, CA: Paw Prints Press, 2009.

Hoogenboom, Lynn. *Juan Ponce de León: A Primary Source Biography.* New York, NY: Rosen Publishing Group 2007. Ebook.

Kling, Andrew A. *The Age of Exploration* (World History Series). Detroit MI: Lucent Books, 2013.

Macdonald, Fiona. *You Wouldn't Want to Sail With Christopher Columbus!: Uncharted Waters You'd Rather Not Cross.* New York, NY: Franklin Watts, 2014.

O'Brien, Cynthia. *Explore With Ponce De León* (Travel With the Great Explorers). New York, NY: Crabtree Publishing, 2015.

Pelleschi, Andrea. *Juan Ponce de León* (Jr. Graphic Famous Explorers). New York, NY: Powerkids Press, 2013.

Pletcher, Kenneth, ed. *The Age of Exploration: From Christopher Columbus to Ferdinand Magellan* (The Britannica Guide to Explorers and Adventurers). New York, NY: Rosen Publishing, 2013.

Rajczak, Michael. *Christopher Columbus* (What You Didn't Know About History). New York, NY: Gareth Stevens, 2015.

Sammons, Sandra Wallus. *Ponce de León and the Discovery of Florida.* Sarasota, FL: Pineapple Press, 2013.

BIBLIOGRAPHY

Allman, T.D. "Ponce de León, Exposed." *New York Times*. April 1, 2013 (http://www.nytimes.com).

Davenport, John, and William H. Goetzmann. *Juan Ponce de León and His Lands of Discovery*. Philadelphia, PA: Chelsea House, 2006.

Francis, J. Michael. "The Fountain of Youth Myth." Think Florida. 2015 (http://www.thinkflorida.org).

Mariner's Museum. "Juan Ponce de León." 2015 (http://ageofex.marinersmuseum.org).

National Park Service. "Fort Jefferson: Dry Tortugas National Park, Florida." Retrieved December 28, 2015 (http://www.nps.gov).

Schimmer, Russell. "Puerto Rico." Yale University. 2015 (http://gsp.yale.edu/case-studies/colonial -genocides-project/puerto-rico).

Schultz, Colin. "Juan Ponce de León's Discovery of Florida." Smithsonian Institute, March 27, 2013 (http://www.smithsonianmag.com).

Slavicek, Louise Chipley. *Juan Ponce de León*. Philadelphia, PA: Chelsea House Publishers, 2003.

Straight, William. "Who Discovered Florida?" Broward County, 2015 (https://www.broward.org/library/ bienes/lii14004.htm).

White, Matthew. *Atrocities: The 100 Deadliest Episodes in Human History.* New York, NY: W.W. Norton & Company, 2013.

INDEX

About the Author

Heather Moore Niver writes and edits all types of books for readers of every age. She has also written biographies about Sojourner Truth, Ruth Bader Ginsberg, and Veronica Roth. Niver lives, writes, and edits in New York State.

Photo Credits